The Search

by

William I. Wickham

The Search

— A Philosophical Ramble —

Foreword

Since this booklet presents my own philosophical thoughts I
initially intended to name it ' *My Search* ' but subsequently deemed
it more appropriate to call it ' *The Search* ' as it seems reasonable to
assume that at some time or other most people have occasion to
ponder the cause and meaning of their existence. As a clergyman
friend of mine from the Western Isles once jocularly remarked " Life
is like a sardine tin, everyone is looking for the key " ; and it seems
to me that for many of us this contains a great deal of truth. Indeed,
this inquiry represents my own attempt to find some sort of answer
to what Fitzgerald's translation of *The Rubaiyat of Omar Khayyam*
refers to as " the quarrel of the Universe " — or rather, on a
somewhat less exalted level, to explore and interpret the meaning of
existence.

On this journey I have, of course, considered and made use of the
answers already proffered by the prominent philosophers of the past.
Spinoza, Hume, Kant, Sartre, Schopenhauer, Russell, Wittgenstein,
and Hegel have all, *inter alia,* supplied the mental food on which I
have sumptuously dined and sought to digest. This has inevitably
meant that this presentation assumes some familiarity with
philosophical notions on the part of the reader — or, rather, it

speaks more readily to those readers who already possess some knowledge of philosophy. And excursions into any social or political implications that my analysis may have have not been excluded. Indeed, I regard all thoughts of relevance to my quest as admissible and welcome and it is my heartfelt hope that the emotional enthusiasm to which I am only too easily prone will not have overwhelmed the reasoning of my mind to a degree that will have sullied my conclusions and rendered them erroneous to the cold eye of logic.

I embark on this task, however, fully conscious of the force of Professor Herbert Feigl's witty observation that ' Philosophy is the disease of which it should be the cure '. In fact, in spite of being of a natural philosophical bent my reason for not choosing philosophy as the subject of my academic studies in my youth was that around the age of sixteen I came to the conclusion that philosophy was a search for truth in which one would never be likely to find it. Nevertheless, at this relatively late stage in my life I now feel impelled to pursue my thoughts on the topic and see where they will lead.

Postscript : Since completing *The Search* I feel, on reflection, that it could be of some interest and use to undergraduate students of philosophy.

I present these thoughts under the following series of headings which have been arranged, as far as possible, in some sort of logical sequence :

1. The human condition and predicament .... Page   1

2. Concerning the theory of knowledge (Epistemology)...... Page   6

3. Concerning the theory of pure being (Ontology).............. Page 18

4. Concerning the Dark Night of Nihilism............................... Page 26

5. Concerning the Metaphysical Realm.................................. Page 28

6. Dawkins Dissected.. Page 34

7. Final Futility and the Mystery... Page 42

1.The human condition and predicament.

I think it was the late Irish comedian Dave Allen who jokingly declared that he was a practising atheist but that on his travels, while staying in various hotels, kept being given a book to read by a fellow called Gideon ; he was referring, of course, to the Bible which, he further alleged, must have been an Irish book because it began at the beginning. With regard to the beginning, one of my earliest memories is of being shown by my father an old Gaelic Bible in which the first line read " Anns an toiseach chruthaich Dia na néamhan agus an talamh " which in English is, of course, " In the beginning God created the heavens and the Earth ". Looking back on that moment from the perspective of the present I am not aware that I had any mental objection at the time to that Biblical assertion, a state of affairs which may have reflected earlier conditioning (or, as some might describe it, " brain washing ") by my mother or simply that it seemed a not unreasonable assumption to make, or, as now seems more likely, an amalgam of both. (I refer here to conditioning by my mother because of an even earlier memory in which she recited to me, while I was a very young child, the traditional prayers " If I should die while I'm asleep, pray the Lord my soul to keep " and " If I should die before I wake, pray the Lord my soul to take " and I distinctly remember being conscious of myself at that time as a living or spiritual entity and, as such, being initially alarmed by the thought that I might die during the night and hoping fervently that if it did happen the Lord, whoever he was, *would* " take " me. In this manner fear and insecurity, if not wisdom, may have been instilled at an early age.) What now seems decidedly unreasonable to me, however, is the stance of those people who always preface their claims with the words " The Bible says " as if that gives them an inviolable authority and validity that is beyond question and without considering or addressing the fact that every word in the Bible has been written by men. Indeed, it was written by a variety of men at different times and in different places, and I am given to understand that the Genesis story was borrowed from the Babylonians. The kind of people who seem to rest their whole case on " the Bible says " do not seem to grasp the fact that if

God created the Universe there cannot possibly be any conflict between the discoveries of scientific investigation and belief in the Deity, and that there is therefore no need to rely on a literal interpretation of the Bible which, in any case, was never intended to be a scientific book. Of course, the standard answer of those people to this challenge is to say that the Bible is " divinely inspired " although they should acknowledge that this does not automatically imply that it has to be read as the literal truth. I personally have written poems which might be said to have been divinely inspired but this is not to say that they express any truth in a literal form. Admittedly, in so far as the Bible expresses goodwill and morally noble intentions we can perhaps legitimately regard it as divinely inspired but it is also possible to view these characteristics as merely the product of socially beneficial necessity or expediency. For example, we can assume that Moses knew full well that for the Israelites to survive their trek across the wilderness after escaping from their Egyptian slavery they would need a set of rules to regulate their behaviour so as to prevent self-destructive anarchy — hence the Ten Commandments. At the same time, however, for those who believe that everything in the Universe originally emanates from a Creator it is possible to view those elements of the Ten Commandments that continue to be a source of social good as basically divinely inspired.

This, of course, raises the fundamental question — *and*, it seems, the perennial problem — of whether or not our existence has emanated from a higher Power and thus invested it with some sort of meaning. Of course, when we consider the Biblical story of Creation as related in the Book of Genesis, we all know in our heart of hearts that some sort of evolution must have taken place because, otherwise, how are we to explain the sudden appearance of Adam without any prior experience ? If, as the Genesis story seems to imply, he emerged on the earthly scene as a fully mature man how would he have come to possess the appropriate experience as he would not have been aware of anything that had gone on before ? (At what age, for example, did he arrive — at 20, 25, 30 or some other arbitrary figure ?) Here I am addressing those Biblical fundamentalists who deny the findings of modern science since even to the eye of commonsense it seems virtually irrefutable that there would have had to have been some sort of evolution. This does not, however, mean that any of us, including Richard Dawkins, really know how or why the process of evolution began in the first place. Since Dawkins makes much of the elegant way in which complex structures developed stage-by-stage from very simple ones he still needs to tell us why the latter began to evolve in the first instance. Clearly, it is quite possible to regard the interaction of energies which must have triggered-off the process as initially inherent in the cosmological framework, so to speak. No one, clever scientist or not, yet knows what gave rise to the Big Bang and nor, therefore, does anyone know for certain why evolution began. We shall return to this topic later.

But whether or not we are believers in a Creator who bestows some sort of meaning to life, the source of all human psychological problems is, in my view, the fact that of all the creatures of the Earth we are the most self-aware, enabling us to anticipate the future and ponder upon the past and present while not knowing with certainty the reason for our emergence, thereby producing insecurity and a related proneness to anxiety. This is the human condition and predicament. It is also the human tragedy because we are all confronted with what the existentialists describe as our ' dreadful freedom ', alleging that we are trapped in a completely meaningless existence with which we are forced to grapple. In my experience, people tend to try and cope with this either by embracing some sort of religious belief or speculating on the " truth " and asking questions about the nature of reality or taking up the practice of meditation or all three ; and from the curiosity which lies at the heart of much of these activities the practise of philosophy is born. When I look at the branches of a particular tree, for example, and the way they are spread out in various directions it is quite obvious to my mind that they could have been laid out differently not only because we know that there exist other trees whose branches are in fact laid out differently but because we are quite capable of imagining that they could be so without in any way challenging or offending our commonsense. As a further step it seems perfectly legitimate to assume that there might be an invisible force behind the reality of the world that could have made that reality appear in a different form ;

but here we run up against the ideas of those philosophers known as extreme empiricists — such as John Stuart Mill and John Henry Newman as well as Hume — who have sought to demonstrate that any such metaphysical notions are meaningless nonsense.

2. Concerning the theory of knowledge (Epistemology).

My first difficulty here lies with the ideas of the Scottish sceptic, David Hume (1711-1776) who has been described as probably being the most influential philosopher of modern times. While I accept Hume's contention that the only meaningful terms or ideas are either sense impressions or mathematical concepts because we have no way of testing the validity of metaphysical propositions I cannot unreservedly embrace his assertion that because our knowledge of causation is basically derived simply from the constant conjunction of associated events we have no adequate evidence for believing that the same sequence of causation will operate in the future. Here I would make a strong plea for the application of commonsense, something that philosophical discourse in general might in many instances have previously benefited from. Hume insists that nothing in our past experience of the uniformity of nature – that is, in the constant association of one event with another such as, for example, a rock striking a window and the ensuing shattering of the glass – gives us any guarantee that the principle of nature's uniformity is true because it is always possible that the future will be different. Even if in the light of our subsequent advances in physics with its awareness of force, momentum and acceleration it may still be the case, as Hume maintains, that we cannot see an entity called *the cause* of an event such as the breaking of the window referred to above, in the same way as we can see, for example, that some object is coloured green it is surely perfectly reasonable for us to assume that a sequence of events which has recurred an incalculable number of times in the past will continue to do so in the future. If it were really possible that it would take a radically different course in the future, then it must surely strengthen my earlier suggestion that the operation of some invisible force would have had to bring this about. At the very least Hume would surely concede that the way in which cause and effect operate in our world is an intrinsic part of its present make-up and is therefore one which on an extremely high balance of probability and without the intervention of some unfamiliar external force is likely to continue to replicate itself in the foreseeable future. The *psychological habits of human nature* upon which Hume claims our expectations and predictions regarding causation are based are on his own admission derived from the inbuilt way in which our Universe is regularly observed to behave and which therefore reveals a physical structure already given.

After all, it can be argued that so-called scientific ' proof ' is merely the extension of experience. We all recognise, for example, that a fire generates heat because up to a certain temperature we can feel the warmth of it simply by placing our hands in front of it and when it gets too hot for us to do this we use an artificially created instrument with an arbitrarily selected scale called a thermometer to *prove* that it is hot. In this way we are proving it merely by employing a man-made instrument which enables us to extend our experience. Is there anything that we can prove in any other way ? One immediately thinks here of arithmetic logic such as we exercise when we say that 1+1 equals 2 ; but is this not also fundamentally based on actual experience ? We *see* a physical object and we count it as 1; we *see* another physical object which, as a single entity, we also specify as 1; but we accord the number 2 to two objects together so that we can then logically demonstrate that 1+1= 2. But the logic here is based on observation and thus on actual experience of the real world as we know it. And is it not the case that even the more sophisticated ' proofs ' furnished by advanced mathematics and modern physics are built upon the foundation of the real world observations which have given rise to arithmetic and maths in the first place and are therefore also derived from our sensory experience ? But what of incontrovertible facts such as the fact that a square will always have four straight lines of equal length or that a triangle will always have three sides ? Well, these shapes with their characteristic properties have been arbitrarily designated by Man as a ' square ' and a ' triangle ' respectively and are both shapes that are *seen* i.e. originally detected *via* our sensory apparatus.

But what of the mathematical philosopher Gottlob Frege's ' concepts ' which he defines as functions whose value for every ' argument ' is a truth-value, an ' argument ' being the particular number inserted into the function — for example, any number used to replace ' x ' in an expression such as $2x^2 + x$? The ' argument 1 ', for instance, would yield the truth-value 3 because replacing x with the number 1 in the expression $2x^2 + x$ gives the result 3. According to Frege, concepts are quite independent of mind or matter because we do not create them ; instead, we discover them but not by the operation of our senses. Put like that, I would, however, challenge this assertion. The existence of our world, and the objects in it, may be a reality that is valid independently of our minds, but our perception of it and our " proving " of it come unavoidably through our senses. The mind may discover and appreciate the truth of a mathematical function and hence of a ' concept ' in Frege's sense but only by first *seeing* or *hearing* its expression. Indeed, I would argue that Frege's claim regarding concepts does not survive deeper scrutiny in terms of our perception of reality. While I accept that concepts as defined by Frege are objective without having the kind of reality that belongs to the physical world of cause and effect, and that the recognition of their truth-value does not depend solely on the operation of our senses [1], they are nevertheless composed of numbers that, fundamentally, have been arbitrarily invented to represent a reality which we can only perceive through our senses. In the abstract, by itself, the number 20, for example, may not be regarded as applying to anything in the real world which impinges

---

[1] *Without the operation of the mind which can perhaps be regarded as a sixth sense.*

on our senses ; but it has fundamentally been derived from having been selected to represent a specific number of objects which our senses have detected as existing in the real world. In fact, none of the concepts herein referred to exist in isolation — which leads me to iterate my first philosophical aphorism in similar form to the declarative statements laid out by Wittgenstein in his *Tractatus* — *Logico Philosophicus* — namely, that ' *Scientific ' proof ' is simply the extension of our general sensory experience* ', and I have deliberately inserted the word ' general ' here to indicate that I am referring to the experience of the bulk of mankind as a whole so as not to be thought to be including in this assertion psychological and/or spiritual experiences which may be real for an individual or group of individuals but not necessarily be of universal validity.

Does this claim on my part mean, however, that I have dismissed or failed to take account of the point put forward by the great philosopher Kant in his *Critique of Pure Reason* that ' although all our knowledge begins with experience, it does not follow that it arises from experience ' ? Kant went on to argue that while our contacts with the experiential world supply the content of our knowledge, our faculties supply the form in which we know it. According to Kant, the form of our experience has an *a priori* character which arises from the mind and not the outside world. We find, for instance, that we neither do have, nor can conceive of, any possible experience except in spatial and temporal terms. Kant claims that in advance of any experience, two kinds of *a priori*

10

characteristics will be present in any awareness that we may have —
namely, that it will have temporal and geometrical features, and that
the truths of mathematics will apply to everything that we discover
about the world of experience.

That the mind does play a part in ordering the form of our
experience is undoubtedly so and Kant's argument here is very
persuasive but in pondering upon the issue I have subjected it to the
following question : ' Why do our minds structure and interpret the
observations of our senses in the way that they do ? Is the form
which they impose upon everything they are in contact with already
inherent in our minds prior to any awareness of our environment
(pre-cognitively present, as it were) because we ourselves are a part
of the world we are experiencing or, as our awareness of the external
world emerges and develops are we unconsciously conditioned by it
through our senses to adopt and impose the spatial and temporal
form which we characteristically bestow on the objects of our
experience ? If we assume the first of these alternative
interpretations as being the case, then, we have to ask how our minds
emerged already armed, as it were, with the blueprint which dictates
the form in which we hold our knowledge of the world. Here we
must resort to the findings of science with regard to evolution and
consider how our minds are thought to have evolved. Given that we
accept that the evolutionary process proceeded gradually over time
via the interaction of our physical bodies with our environment it
must inevitably have involved sensory experience and on this basis it

is reasonable to maintain that the contribution our minds make to the form in which we have knowledge of the world stems basically, either consciously or unconsciously, from the intake of our senses. Otherwise we have to conclude that the mind is some sort of freewheeling entity that emerges without any dependence on, or connection with, the physical body with which it is associated and from which it presumably springs — surely a ridiculous proposition ! ? If we follow this line of interpretation we will be back with the mind-body division of Cartesian dualism which modern philosophy has subsequently tended to discredit.

Admittedly, it is much more difficult to discount the purely cognitive character of mathematical propositions. Unlike a simple statement such as ' the table is white ' a mathematical truth is not subject to the inaccuracies of sensory perception or the differences in individual perceptions of reality. The truth of propositions such as $1+1=2$ or $2x^2 + x = S$ (where S stands for the resultant number) is universally recognizable without any equivocation. Why is this ? Isn't it because we first understand what the numbers are, and we understand what the numbers are because we know that they represent a visible series of items or objects. We can count them by *seeing* them ; in other words, through the use of one of our senses. Again, take, for example, a slightly more obscure calculation, 5 x 5. We know that this comes to 25 through our knowledge of what is called ' the multiplication table ' which we have previously memorised. It may seem that no sensory experience is needed in order to grasp its truth although it should be noted that we have at some stage had to see or hear the expression ' 5 x 5 ' in order to be able to perform the calculation in our minds. We have also needed to feel confident that the numbers involved accurately represent a succession of items or objects in the real world which, if required, we could count by seeing or touching them i.e. through sensory data.

So the cognitive purity of mathematical truths can be seen as a sort of superstructure built upon a foundation of sensory experience. It derives basically from Man's attempt to represent reality in symbolic form. It is this symbolic abstraction which, I submit, makes mathematical statements seem to convey more certain knowledge than that derived from observations such as ' The table is white '. If we so wish, this sentence can, for example, be represented by mathematical symbols [2] but that will not alter the fact that its basic meaning will be subject to the imperfections and variance of individuals' perceptions. From the top of the superstructure one cannot readily see its foundation but without the foundation it is meaningless. Comprehensible perhaps but without significance.

Incidentally, I have suddenly realised that I have been writing in direct opposition to the position taken by Wittgenstein in his *Tractatus* as I am given to understand that he maintained that logic (through language) came before experience whereas I have been

---

[2] *E.g. we could represent the statement " the table is white " by xp where x is the subject of the sentence and p its predication.*

implying that logic was built on experience. Indeed, I would argue that the development of language stems originally from peoples' response to their sense-data i.e. to their sensory experience of the external world. As groupings of people, or tribes or races, felt impelled to communicate with each other they obviously would have had to represent objects in their respective environments with sounds that were acceptable to the whole group in question and this must at some stage have involved one or more of them inventing or selecting, in accordance with their social culture and physical structure, words to reflect their sensory experience of their external world.

But at this point I am aware of the fact that my argument here rests wholly on my earlier assertion that the natural processes by which we and our minds evolved unconsciously involved the development of our sensory experience which, in turn, is the cause of our *a priori* knowledge of the world to which Kant was referring when he described such knowledge as **forms of intuition.** If my contention is sound I am refuting Kant's argument that we human beings can possess knowledge that is independent of experience and reasserting the basic primacy of sensory data [3]. And such a contention has another off-shoot which I feel compelled to spell out here. Knowledge that a genetic inheritance has been bestowed on us by the process of evolution has always caused me to have misgivings about

Jean-Paul Sartre's well-known statement that ' existence precedes essence '. Sartre's notion that Man is completely free to adopt his own project i.e. free to decide how he reacts to his environment and therefore solely responsible for what he will become has always seemed to me to deny the fact that we each inherit certain genes which heavily influence how we react to the environment in which we find ourselves. Since our genetic inheritance must at least influence, if not completely determine, the way in which we respond to our environment I cannot accept, as Sartre seems to suggest, that Man is completely free to decide what he will become and is solely responsible for it. But in deference to the likelihood that Sartre understood this and did not therefore mean that Man was free in the sense in which I have interpreted his words — although on the basis of his writings it is hard to assume any other interpretation — I have adopted, and seek here to assert, a contrary claim in the form of the following aphorism : ' *Essence accompanies existence* ', or, more accurately perhaps, ' *Existence and essence emerge together* '.

In any case, I am aware that an attentive reader will probably have noticed at this point that the arguments I have been putting forward,

---

3 *Since the time of writing I have become aware that to a certain extent my disagreement with Kant here seems similar to some of the criticisms levelled against his reasoning by the philosopher Schopenhauer in Volume 1 of his book ' The World as Will and Representation '. Although he agrees with Kant that knowledge can come from a priori intuition or perception that is independent of experience, he seems, at the same time, to concur with what I have been trying say in the following sentence taken from page 41 of his book : ' For the whole world of reflection rests on the world of perception as its ground of knowledge '.*

and the aphorism with which I have summed them up on page 10,
vindicates the extreme empiricism which I previously seemed poised
to challenge insofar as it implied that the metaphysical propositions
put forward by traditional philosophy are meaningless nonsense.
Indeed, this view was further reinforced by the more recently
developed philosophies known as Logical Atomism and Logical
Positivism. The first of these was based on Bertrand Russell's
assumption that the symbolic logic developed in his great work on
mathematical logic, *Principia Mathematica* (1910-1913), gave us
the sketch of a perfect language because it mirrored the structure of
the actual world. The contention was that when a sentence of
ordinary English was translated into its logical form its meaning
could be unravelled ; and if, on such translation, it turned out to be
of the subject-predicate form (in its logical but not necessarily its
grammatical presentation) it constituted what Russell called an
' atomic proposition ' because it would contain no separate parts
which were themselves propositions and would denote an actual
object in the real world and its characteristics or properties. In other
words, by analysing the sentences of natural languages so as to put
them into their proper logical form, their meaning would become
clear and philosophical perplexity thereby eliminated. Roughly
speaking, through such analysis, philosophy would tell us that the
world is composed of a set of atomic facts i.e. objects and their
properties. Yet Logical Atomism is still regarded as a metaphysical
system in the traditional sense insofar as it holds that philosophy is

an activity which gives us knowledge about the structure of the world, albeit not the same kind of knowledge as science gives. It was superseded by Logical Positivism which was thought to have been initiated in the 1920's by a remark of the philosopher Wittgenstein to the effect that philosophy is not a theory but an activity. A group of thinkers known as the ' Vienna Circle ' elaborated upon this view and concluded that philosophy does not produce propositions which are true or false but merely clarifies the meaning of statements, showing some to be scientific, some to be mathematical and some (including most so-called philosophical statements) to be nonsensical. According to this viewpoint, every significant statement is either a statement of formal logic (in the broad sense of *Principia Mathematica* and thus including mathematical statements) or a statement of science broadly interpreted to include not only statements of physical laws but also singular sentences such as ' This is white '. All other types of statement were not cognitive and were therefore, strictly speaking, nonsensical ; if they had any meaning at all it was described as ' poetical ' or ' emotive ' or ' pictorial ' or ' motivational '.

When considering all these theories, being conscious of the meaningfulness of their attempts to " bore down ", as it were, on reality in order to see what could be accepted with certainty, I myself pondered over what significance a simple basic English sentence such as, for example, ' This table is white ' would convey. I recognised immediately, of course, that this sentence fitted in with

Wittgenstein's Picture Theory that a perfect language (as sketched by Russell in the *Principia*) pictured or mirrored the structure of reality because its subject, a table, corresponded with an actual entity in the real world while its predicate, ' is white ', denoted an actual characteristic of that table. But I also realised at once that this simple sentence does not convey an absolutely accurate picture of reality for the simple reason that it does not tells us, for example, whether we are talking about a ' big ' table, a ' small ' table or a ' normal ', or ' average ', or ' ordinary-sized ' table which are characteristics that might in any case depend on the relative sizes of different viewers of the reality in question. Again, while we can accept that the table's colour is ' white ' because most of mankind would agree that that is what it is we cannot be entirely sure as to how white it is ; is it ' very ' white or only ' mildly ' white, for example ? Obviously, the degree of whiteness which we ascribe to the table can also vary from person to person. These reflections have led me to declare my second aphorism — ' *Everything is relative to us and we are relative to everything* '. Of course, this idea is not new, but nevertheless it seems to me to be irrefutably true.

3. Concerning the theory of pure being (Ontology).

While I acknowledge and appreciate the contribution which the philosophies outlined in 2. above have made to our understanding of the world and the rôle of philosophy in relation to it, I feel that I have to make the observation that they are purely engaged in the philosophical equivalent of ' navel-gazing '. We are all surely aware that we can attempt to break down the external world into atomic propositions and facts. We can " bore down ", as it were, into the physical world to isolate and examine its fundamental constituents. We can even go so far as to pursue science in its search for the Higgs boson or so-called ' God ' particle in the hope of attaining a better understanding of how the Big Bang spawned our Universe (although if we do, I suspect we may end up in the same quandary as that alluded to at the end of the limerick that I have entitled *Black Holes* and reproduced below on page 20). But I would dare to suggest that this is not what we — both ordinary people and philosophers — are really looking for. We are looking for the meaning and purpose of existence and how this should perhaps condition our mental state, and in this connection it is probably a great mistake for philosophy to exclude or dismiss consideration of those statements which the Vienna Circle (see above) described as being non-cognitive and therefore ' poetical ', or ' emotive ' or ' pictorial ' or ' motivational '. After all, our immediate reaction to, and puzzlement about, the world we are born into does not normally take the form of a search for mathematical or symbolic logic or atomistic propositions. When we see before us, for example, a beautiful, grass-covered mountain our response to it, and the queries it may evoke in us, are in fact likely to be more accurately described as ' poetical ' or ' mystical ' as opposed to logical or mathematical. It is surely true to say that in general, at first sight, we humans take cognisance of the world as it presents itself to us as a whole rather than as a conglomeration of mathematical symbols or atomic propositions.

What I am trying to contend in the previous paragraph is that the curiosity which evokes philosophical thinking in the first place is our reaction to the totality of that part of the external world of which we are aware. Moreover, we are surely trying to adopt an interpretation of reality with which we may perhaps condition our state of mind, and for this reason we may have to readmit into our serious thinking those ideas which the Logical Positivists of the Vienna Circle described in a dismissive vein as ' poetical ' or ' emotive ' or ' pictorial ' or ' motivational '. When I stated earlier in connection with my first aphorism that I had deliberately employed the word

Black Holes

From macro to micro inside a black hole,
To merge gravity with quantum mechanics,
The physicists puzzle
And the scientists struggle
To come up with a theory that's whole.

Let them look toward CERN if they're eager to learn
What gravity does down the hole,
For the Hadron Collider
Might show what's inside her,

And play an astonishing rôle.

But have they considered the large and the small

May not be designed to embrace,

So is it time to admit

That a Creator might fit

In the holes they've discovered in Space ?

Even if they come up with a theory complete

Will they ever be able to know

Why a star is born out of nothing

And in time disappears in a glow ?

' general ' in order to exclude personal psychological experiences
which might be valid for some but not for others I did not mean that
we should necessarily regard these as unimportant. Indeed, what can
be more important to us in our lives than our state of mind ? St. Paul,
for example, was driven by a certain state of mind born of his
religious background and his related ' conversion ' on the road to
Damascus, an experience which eventually turned the world upside
down, so to speak, by leading to the adoption of Christianity as the
official religion of the Roman Empire. Hitler — whom Churchill
aptly described as ' a maniac of ferocious genius ' — was mentally
imbued with a conviction which fired a kind of secular religion that
led to all the destruction and suffering of the Second World War.
Few in Europe, including the philosopher Jean Paul Sartre, were
unaffected by its effects. I seem to remember reading somewhere

also that Bertrand Russell at the age of around 90 declared that he had discovered that he no longer loved his wife. I cannot help asking myself ' What did he mean by ' love ' ' ? Presumably he was referring to what he himself would have agreed was a ' state of mind '. As a professed atheist, who seems to have reduced our knowledge of the world to mathematical logic — or, rather, failed to do so because of his discovery of a paradox at the heart of Gottlob Frege's fifth axiom of logic [4]— how did he explain this condition of ' love ' which was obviously of some importance to him. ? Does this not point to the need for philosophical thinking to adopt a wider perspective ? Even the philosophical searching which arrives at a restrictive view of reality by imposing logical limits to our epistemology must surely exert an influence on the outlook and attitude of those philosophers who accept these findings. Did not Wittgenstein, for example, ultimately come to view philosophy as a therapeutic activity ? And better perhaps than ' poetical ' as a description of a person's possible view of the world in which he finds himself, as suggested above, is the word ' aesthetic ' because I

---

[4] *This refers to the fact that if the class of all classes that are not members of themselves (e.g. the class of dogs is not itself a dog) is a member of itself (as it must be) then it cannot be the class of those classes and if it is not a member of itself then it is the class of all classes that are not members of themselves. Russell attempted to avoid this paradox by claiming that it was wrong to treat classes as randomly classifiable objects but Frege's definition of the series of natural numbers required the assumption that the number of objects in the Universe is infinite and the lack of a logical basis for this postulate seems to nullify Russell's attempt to derive arithmetic from logic alone.*

for one sometimes instinctively feel impelled to view the Earth on which we live, with its marvellously inspiring mountains and lush greenery, as a ' work of art ' often leading me to fancy that if there is an invisible Creator responsible for it He was, in his act of creation, expressing himself in some sort of creative orgasm or artistic display.

At this point I am aware that the reader will feel that I have gone from one end of the philosophical spectrum to the other, so to speak, by embracing notions which obviously breach the cognitive limit apparently imposed by the extreme empiricism which my previous arguments supported. I should, however, point out in passing that I am not proposing such an extreme degree of empiricism as that associated with Bishop Berkeley who reputedly implied that if an object was not presently detectible by our senses (e.g. not at the moment being looked at, or heard, or touched, or smelt) then it did not exist. When I argue that our knowledge of the external world comes through our sensory experience I definitely do not mean that we thereby *know* the real nature of the substances underlying the entities in the external world which make up our sense-data. Science has made us only too aware that the objects we see around us can be broken down into molecules and atoms which can be further broken down into sub-atomic particles whose behaviour we are not entirely certain about and which can perhaps be further broken down ad infinitum. I recognise and accept the Einsteinian-based claim of science that matter is arrested energy. We are touching here upon infinity and my earlier arguments concerning sensory experience are in no way claiming that our senses give us definite knowledge of the true or exact nature of the external world in which we find ourselves ; simply that our awareness of our external world, such as it is, unavoidably comes initially via our senses. Indeed, my reference here to the knowledge that science has furnished us with helps explain why I do not believe that science should be excluded from the purview of philosophy as some modern philosophers have sought to maintain any more than I wish to exclude those ways of viewing things that I have outlined in the previous paragraph. For me science forms an indispensable part of philosophical enquiry rather in similar vein to the way Wittgenstein claimed that the paragraphs of his *Tractatus* provided a ladder which must be thrown away after one had climbed it if one wanted to see the world aright. By contrast, however, I do not advocate that we should throw the ladder of science away but that one should be free, if one so wishes, to jump off the end of this ladder by indulging in instinctive speculation about the fundamental meaning and purpose of our Universe and our place within it.

Before the reader thinks that I have now completely abandoned any philosophical rigour or discipline let me state categorically that I concur with the Verifiability Criterion of Meaning developed by the Logical Positivists as a test of what is significant in a factual sense concerning our knowledge of the world. I accept that in the present state of our knowledge none of the speculations that I might entertain as to what might lie behind our known Universe or what might have brought it into existence can possibly be the subject of scientific verification. But does this mean that we cannot on any account be permitted to make commonsense assumptions on the basis of probability ? In other words, we are denied the constructive use of imagination. I would suggest that the mathematicians and logicians have overlooked one simple point — namely, that we do not really need mathematics or logic to tell us that our factual knowledge of the world is confined to our knowledge of whatever it is that exists, to that which ' *is* '. But are we on that account to discount the exercise of commonsense speculation ? If the circumstances warrant it a group of people can, for example, believe it likely that a friend of theirs is standing round a particular corner even if it turns out not to be so. Of course, I recognise that the difference between this kind of expectation and a metaphysical assumption that there is a creative Power behind the Universe is that we already have evidence of what a person is like and that he is capable of existence, of actually being there, whereas we have no concrete proof that there is an invisible force responsible for the Universe or any knowledge of what such a force might be like. Nevertheless, we may concede that speculation about this might have more philosophical legitimacy once we have contemplated the content of the next section.

4. Concerning the Dark Night of Nihilism.

Let us suppose that there is no hidden or underlying explanation for the existence of the Universe, no force or power that created it, no meaning or purpose to its existence, no rational reason or succour for our individual lives within it and that in the words of Matthew Arnold

" we are here as on a darkling plain
Swept with confused alarms of struggle and flight,
Where ignorant armies clash by night ".

One problem with our possible acceptance of this state of affairs, however, is that we have to acknowledge that the Universe seems to be subject to the constant operation of Motion, that Motion is, as I think Thomas Hobbs maintained, an inherent principle of the Universe. This evokes a natural curiosity, in me at least, as to how *the direction* of the motion of the various entities visible within our Universe is determined. What decides whether a planet, or for that matter a cell, moves in one direction as opposed to another ? Of course, we know that direction can only be precisely ascertained in relation to the location of the observer. But irrespective of the restrictive framework imposed by our actual location in Space what determines whether a body moves in one direction or another ? Even if we did not exist and could not therefore state in which direction a body was moving in relation to us what would determine its *direction* of movement ? Why should it go one way and not another ? Of course, we know that everything in the Universe is connected with everything else and that the movement of one entity in a particular direction must in all probability be determined in some way by its associated entities or forces, but where is our starting point ? What is the overall determinant of the motion of a particular entity (such as a star, a planet, a cloud or even a cell, for example) in a particular direction ?

At this point, in my reasoning, we run into the concept of the ' infinite regress ' which the scientist Richard Dawkins has used as an argument against the notion of a prime mover called God, alleging that an assumption that there is a God merely begs the question of what caused his existence and so on *ad infinitum*. But not being, by his own admission in his book *The God Delusion*, a philosopher, he does not entertain the possibility that an infinitely creative spirit may underlie the existence of the Universe as opposed to a blind inorganic piece of matter devoid of any conscious energy, mind or will. It has long been a facet of my thinking that as far as an explanation for the existence of the Universe is concerned the choice must ultimately lie between acceptance that an infinitely creative spirit is at work — that is, a spirit or energy which, with our finite minds, is ' beyond our ken ' so to speak — or that it is primarily the product of an item of ' dead ' inorganic matter ; or are these just two sides of the same coin, as Spinoza would have said, with the Spirit expressing itself through and *within* the physical Universe we see around us, something which Dawkins seems unwilling to contemplate as a possibility because there is no evidence of its existence in a physical sense ?

At this juncture I would present today's philosophers with a plea on behalf of commonsense. I beg leave of modern empiricist philosophy to permit some commonsense speculation about the metaphysical realm for as some Arab mystic once said " It is better to light a candle than to curse the darkness ".

5. Concerning the Metaphysical Realm.

Despite what modern empiricist philosophers may say it is surely only natural for an ordinary human being to wonder why something exists. Take, for example, a Sun. Why is there such an entity as a Sun ? The scientists will tell us that it consists of ' nuclear reactions ' but what does this really mean ? They can doubtless explain how it came about, but why does it exist at all ? I defy anyone, scientist or not, to give us a satisfactory answer.

While I am fully aware that some prominent modern philosophers regard any metaphysical propositions as meaningless, they should also reflect on the ridiculousness of the stance taken by those atheistic scientists who in their eagerness to proclaim that there is no evidence to substantiate a belief in a Creator invite us to believe in magic insofar as they seem to imply — in contradiction to their much vaunted rationality — that the Big Bang happened without a cause. Not something an ordinary person would normally accept. To be fair, however, a scientist such as Richard Dawkins would probably maintain that what he is saying is that he is not aware of any physical evidence of a cause of the Big Bang while, as I understand it, Stephen Hawking's latest take on the subject is that the occurrence of the Big Bang can probably be explained *via* the operation of some physical gravitational law which perhaps brought our known Universe out of the invisible Dark Matter of which, together with Dark Energy, most of it is apparently made up. Who or what framed this law is, of course, another matter. Indeed, could it be perhaps that it is in this Dark Matter and Dark Energy in which, unbeknown to us, in the words of the New Testament, " we live and move and have our being " ?

We should be careful to bear in mind that because the existence of something cannot be verified does not provide a sound reason for concluding that it does not exist. Imagine two computers talking to each other about whether there is someone who made them. A computer has the ability to perform complex tasks at a speed that is far beyond the capability of Man but is nevertheless totally unaware of its creator's existence. Those two computers which I have imagined communicating with each other would be perfectly justified in concluding that there was no evidence that anyone had made them. Yet, irrefutably, we, the inventors of the computer, do actually exist.

Again, when we look down on the ants running about underneath our feet on a hot summer's day we instinctively know, without any concrete evidence or scientific proof, that they are unaware of our existence. As far as they are concerned, but seemingly unbeknown to them, we inhabit a different dimension. [5] And how many dimensions are there ? We already know that the atom, invisible to our naked eye, resembles a mini-solar system and consists of even smaller subatomic particles. So even within our own Universe there seems to be numerous dimensions.

By way of a brief digression here it is interesting to consider certain aspects of modal logic which is the branch of logic dealing with the notions of necessity and possibility[56]. The key idea of modern modal logic — which was made respectable by the work of a number of logicians in the early 1960's — is to exploit the similarities between quantification (i.e. the logical use in sentences of words such as ' some ' and ' all ') and modalities (i.e. modes of truth) by defining ' necessity ' as truth in all possible worlds, and ' possibility ' as truth in some possible world. Plain truth is then thought of as truth in the actual world, which is one among all possible worlds. The semantics involved here are illustrated by

---

5 *At this point I cannot help remembering with amusement the following verse quoted to me by my father in the Scottish vernacular :*
" Crawling aboot like a snail in the grass
Covered in clammy clay,
Me — made after the image of God,
Jings, but it's laughable tae ! ".

considering a universe in which there are just two objects, *a* and *b*,
and three predicates, *F*, *G* and *H* and by supposing that in that
universe there are, as shown below, three possible worlds, of which
world 2 is the actual one, which we may call alpha, and where the
symbol ~ denotes negation i.e. ' not '

World 1   *Fa*   *~Ga*   *~Ha*   *~Fb*   *Gb*   *Hb*

World 2   *Fa*   *~Ga*   *Ha*   *~Fb*   *Gb*   *~Hb*

World 3   *Fa*   *Ga*   *~Ha*   *Fb*   *Gb*   *Hb*

Now if necessity is truth in all possible worlds, we have in this
universe ' Necessarily Fa ' and ' Necessarily Gb '. The modality
expressed by ' If necessarily p, then p ' is exemplified by the truth
of *Fa* and *Gb* in alpha, the actual world. If possibility is truth in some
possible world we have, for example, ' Possibly *Fb* ' and ' Possibly
Ga ', even though Fb and Ga are false in alpha.

There are many such statements that can be formulated within
modal logic about whose truth value there is no consensus among

6 *The ensuing discussion over Pages 30-32 draws heavily on the material
provided by Volume 4, pp.116-120 of ' Philosophy in the Modern World ' by Sir
Anthony Kenny, first published in 2007 by the Oxford University Press.*

logicians. The most contentious ones are those in which modal operators are iterated : for example, the two following formulae :

If possibly possibly p, then possibly p

If necessarily p, then necessarily necessarily p

This iteration of modalities is now explained in terms of a relationship to be defined between different possible worlds. One possible world may or may not be accessible from another. When we use a single operator, as in ' possibly p', we can be taken to be saying ' In some possible world beta, accessible from alpha, p is the case '. But it cannot be taken for granted that every world accessible from beta is also accessible from alpha, and talk of possible worlds need not involve any metaphysical implications.

Nonetheless, these aspects of the logic of necessity and possibility are illuminating in view of the fact that the latest thinking in the field of astrophysics, as I understand it, involves what is termed String theory which postulates the possible existence of eleven different dimensions or parallel Universes. Yet this theory has none of the concrete evidence that Richard Dawkins appears to demand as the essential measure of scientific truth, and despite the claims of some of the modern philosophical logicians that metaphysical propositions are meaningless we have to recognise that with String theory the astrophysicists of today are engaged in nothing less than mathematical metaphysical speculation. If we accept Dawkins' need of solid scientific evidence, can any scientist deny it ? So not only is my plea for a broader, all-encompassing philosophy that permits commonsense speculation on the mysteries of the Universe not so misguided perhaps as some of the more mathematically oriented philosophers of the past century have implied, but such speculation is in fact currently taking place on the modern frontiers of scientific investigation, albeit through the medium of sophisticated mathematics.

Strangely enough, someone whose writings do seem in some sense to have a definite philosophical similarity to these modern investigations are those of the German philosopher Hegel (1770 1831), as may perhaps be detected from the following extracts from an analytical commentary by J. N. Findlay on the Preface to Hegel's great work *Phenomenology of Spirit*, particularly in the second paragraph (i.e. 34) shown below —

" 33. Ancient thought differs from ours in that it built directly on the natural consciousness, and reached out to the universal from it, whereas our thought finds the universal ready to hand, in hard, fixed form, which it then has to revitalize and restore to fluidity. So vitalized, fixed ideas become self-moving notions, spiritual essentialities.

34. Such a movement of pure essentialities is Science as such, whose content is nothing but their necessary expansion into an organic whole. The notion of Science does not arise out of contingent

philosophizing on these or those themes, relations or common ideas, nor from logical manipulations of these or those definite thoughts, but from the rounding-itself-out of the self-moving concept into cosmic completeness. "

6. Dawkins Dissected.

I cannot help but wonder what Richard Dawkins thinks about those above-mentioned modern mathematical speculations in view of his apparent insistence on hard evidence. I certainly cannot accept his assertion — which appears on page 18 of his book *The God Delusion* — that " pantheism is sexed-up atheism " in view of its implication that Spinoza — who, after all, based his philosophical thesis on the best scientific foundation available at the time, namely, the propositions of Euclid – was an atheist which he decidedly was not judging by his declaration that God was a substance consisting of infinite attributes and without whom nothing could be conceived.

I think it would be difficult, however, for anyone to disagree with Dawkins' observations about traditional ideas of God and religion as described in the Old Testament and his criticisms of the way in which the children of various faith groups are indoctrinated with such ideas, but, this aside, his main case concerning the Universe and our existence within it seems to rest on what he refers to as ' the anthropic principle '. By this I understand him to mean that if there is a sufficiently large number of galaxies in the Universe — as there undoubtedly is − then the apparently improbable and fortuitous location of our solar system in the so-called ' Goldilocks zone ' where ' six fundamental constants ' of the Universe appear to be so finely tuned as to permit the emergence and evolution of Life is not so remarkable as some scientists deem it to be. It is essentially a statistical argument. In his own words, " It has been estimated that there are between 1 billion and 30 billion planets in our galaxy, and about 100 billion galaxies in the Universe. Knocking a few noughts off for reasons of ordinary prudence, a billion billion is a conservative estimate of the number of available planets in the Universe. If the odds of life originating spontaneously on a planet were a billion to one against, nevertheless that stupefyingly improbable event would still happen on a billion planets ..... even a chemical model with odds of success as low as one in a billion would *still* predict that life would arise on *one* in a billion billion to give us a good and entirely satisfying explanation for the presence of life here. " Although one would normally think that a rational scientist would, on a balance of probability, regard the unique settings of the six fundamental constants as unlikely to have been the result of chance and as evidence of deliberate intention on the part of some sort of intelligence, the ' anthropic principle ', as elucidated by Dawkins, permits him − quite legitimately in statistical terms − to circumvent this apparently logical standpoint. However, this principle begs the question of why the astronomical number of galaxies arose in the first place. As Dawkins himself acknowledges, we do not as yet have a satisfactory explanation for the existence of the Universe of the kind provided by Darwinism for biological evolution on our own planet ; but he suggests that some sort of equivalent ' crane ', capable of ' working up gradually and plausibly from simplicity to otherwise improbable complexity ', could in principle do for physics the same explanatory work as Darwinism does for biology ; and he suggests further that some kind of multiverse theory, abetted by the anthropic principle, might provide it.

At this point I have to say that I cannot for the life of me see what is simple about the idea of a multiverse. I also note that with a scientist's typical precision Dawkins seems to assume that believers in a Creator automatically view him as someone who sits down, as it were, and consciously and deliberately designs things in all their evident complexity whereas he may simply, when giving rise to our visible Universe, have been expressing himself in a kind of orgasm of artistic creation in much the same way as an artist spontaneously releases his subconscious strivings without necessarily knowing in advance what the detailed outcome is going to be.

In connection with this topic, by way of a brief diversion, the following passage from Schopenhauer's *World as Will and Representation* casts an interesting sidelight —
" But now, what kind of knowledge is it that considers what continues to exist outside and independently of all relations, but

alone which is really essential to the world, the true content of its phenomena, that which is subject to no change, and is therefore known with equal truth for all time, in a word, the Ideas [7] that are the immediate and adequate objectivity of the thing-in-itself, of the will ? It is *art*, the work of genius. It repeats the eternal Ideas apprehended through pure contemplation, the essential and abiding element in all the phenomena of the world. According to the material in which it repeats, it is sculpture, painting, poetry, or music. Its only source is knowledge of the Ideas ; its sole aim is communication of this knowledge. Whilst science, following the restless and unstable stream of the fourfold forms of reasons or grounds and consequents, is with every end it attains again and again directed farther, and can never find an ultimate goal or complete satisfaction, any more than by running we can reach the point where the clouds touch the horizon ; art, on the contrary, is everywhere at its goal. For it plucks the object of its contemplation from the stream of the world's course, and holds it isolated before it. This particular thing, which in that stream was an infinitesimal part, becomes for art a representative of the whole, an equivalent of the infinitely many in space and time. It therefore pauses at this particular thing ; it stops the wheel of time ; for it the relations vanish ; its object is only the essential, the Idea. We can therefore define it accurately as *the way of considering*

7 *Plato's famous concept of the reality that lies behind all the visible phenomena of the Universe (my footnote).*

things independently of the principle of sufficient reason [8], in contrast to the way of considering them which proceeds in exact accordance with this principle, and is the way of science and experience. This latter method of consideration can be compared to an endless line running horizontally, and the former to a vertical line cutting the horizontal at any point. ..."

I am aware, of course, that Richard Dawkins is, by his own admission, not a philosopher but a scientist. The chief obstacle to his belief in a Creator seems to be the concept of the infinite regress with which our reason has to grapple if we presuppose a God with the intelligence to create the improbable complexity of our Universe. In other words, if God explains the latter, how do we explain God, and so on *ad infinitum* ? But this line of enquiry tends to treat God as if he must be on our own level. How, for instance, does a complex computer explain its inventor when it is not even aware of him ? Of course, a scientist such as Dawkins would immediately point out that a computer is an inorganic piece of material which is pre-programmed to do all the wonderful things it can do and that therefore the analogy is not a legitimate one. But is there really a difference in this sense between an inorganic assembly of metal and circuit boards and the various components of our Universe ? Other than biological life on our own planet, both consist of inorganic

---

8 *According to* Schopenhauer, *the* general *meaning of this principle is that always and everywhere each thing exists merely by virtue of another thing " or, as he states it differently, " nothing is without a ground or a reason why it is ".*

material, do they not ? And as to the infinite regress, I feel compelled to mention at this point that long before I ever heard of Richard Dawkins or read his book *The God Delusion* I had come to the conclusion, in pondering the origin of our Universe, that there was a choice between believing in an infinite creative Spirit (or energy) [9] or an original piece, in some form, of inorganic material devoid of any intentional impetus, will or mind. If we opt for belief in the latter then we have no way of explaining the Big Bang other than through an inexplicable accident that completely contravenes scientific causality and logic — tantamount in fact to an irrational belief in magic ! And if we leave open, as I do, the possibility of the former, the implication must surely be that the infinite regress to which Dawkins refers and which poses such a problem for him is synonymous in fact with this infinitely creative Spirit which must therefore be operative or inherently present in a way which cannot be openly detected by us by means of the scientific evidence and investigation normally relied upon by we human beings any more than an ant crawling about on a hot summer's day is aware of us or anymore than a computer is conscious of its inventor (after all, modern science now tells us that there may be as many as 11 dimensions !). In a sense this concept is expressed in the following lines which I penned while a student at Edinburgh University during

[9] *Rather along the lines of the description given in the Westminster Shorter Catechism that ' God is a Spirit, infinite, eternal and unchangeable.*

the 1960's :

Continuously creative, circularly circling

Comes the great Spirit called God,

Of the familiar Universe He is the measuring rod,

Not out of nothing but out of Him it came

And He is infinity just the same.

His Cause, his Creator, and his Creator's cause

Are just infinity without any Laws

To which matter, dead matter, alone is subjected,

By which planets in Space alone are connected.

I realise, of course, that Dawkins would reject the notion that a
Spirit was operative in an indetectible way on the grounds that there
was no physical evidence of the existence of such a force or entity
but before the reader rushes to agree with him it is worthwhile noting
that even his much-vaunted use of logic can sometimes slip up as is
evident from the following extract from page 86 of his book *The God
Delusion* where he is refuting the argument that beautiful works of art
imply the existence of God :

" Obviously Beethoven's late quartets are sublime. So are
Shakespeare's sonnets. They are sublime if God is there and they are
sublime if he isn't. They do not prove the existence of God ; *they
prove the existence of Beethoven and of Shakespeare.* (my italics) "
Wrong. Strictly speaking, they manifestly do not prove with absolute
certainty the existence of Beethoven and of Shakespeare, as the well

known doubts and disputes over the authorship of the latter's plays surely demonstrates. Can anyone deny that there are still those who contend that Shakespeare's plays were actually written by Marlowe [10] ? The existence of those quartets and sonnets does not *prove* the existence of Beethoven and Shakespeare. How can we be certain beyond any doubt that they were not written by other authors ?

What the existence of those quartets and sonnets does do, however — and I think this is what Dawkins really meant — is provide evidence that they had human creators ; just as, to my mind, the existence of the Universe furnishes evidence of a divine Creator.

And I cannot help observing that Dawkins seems to show the same ardour and zeal in attacking belief in God as religious fundamentalists portray in proclaiming it, an aspect of his activity which inevitably gives me the impression that he is struggling to escape from, and overcome, as it were, the influence of his own religious upbringing. Even if this assessment of his attitude is unjust I am perturbed by a story recently related to me by a student friend that Dawkins wrote to an academic who had just been appointed to the position of Professor of Theology that he should resign his post as Theology was a non-subject. Given that he cannot possibly be 100% certain that there is no God, and that such an action is in any case unnecessary, this certainly seems to smack of the arrogance which

[10] *Christopher Marlowe, an English dramatist and poet of the Elizabethan era.*

some of my acquaintances have accused him of.

7. Final Futility and The Mystery.

I have just finished reading Leo Tolstoy's remarkable book, *The Gospel in Brief,* and while one has to admire the fact that he seemed ahead of his time in the way in which this work deliberately ignored the mythology, history and official representation in which Christianity had become encrusted and concentrated solely on the words allegedly spoken by Christ himself and the central kernel of his message, because of Tolstoy's claim in his Introduction that Jesus had replaced the belief in an external God by the belief that a true ' understanding of life is God ' I cannot help being left with a feeling that this implies that there is no after-life of which one's soul can be consciously aware of and that therefore Christ went to his death for nothing and that there was no real purpose in it. However, I think Tolstoy's own interpretation of the Gospel is that if one can live in the spirit rather than the flesh then the fear of death will be removed or at least mitigated and the moment of its occurrence does not matter because at that point one will be united with the universal spirit underlying the Universe, a viewpoint rather similar, I suppose, to Spinoza's pantheistic conception of existence. As is stated in the introduction to the last Chapter of Tolstoy's book " The death of the body is union with the Father ". The concept expressed here is in a

sense inherent in the following lines which were inspired in me one
evening by the practice of meditation.

Blissful Oblivion
Meditation's theme tonight
Is full annihilation,
Hollow, hollow emptiness,
The aim of meditation ;
For nothing brings us something
As something comes from nothing,
And ' maranatha ', ' maranatha ',
Our meditation chant,
The anodyne for stress and strife
Will in our souls implant ;
For life's grim ills we use the balm
Of Oriental leaven,
And when our cells disintegrate
And slip into the void,
If there be no after-life
But only blind oblivion,
This be the bliss of angels,
The everlasting heaven.

I completed this poem with only a residue of what might be classed
as the infantile hope [11] that our souls might experience some sort of

11 *i.e. drawn from childhood inculcation*

consciousness of existence after death as seems to be implied by the Biblical verse ' Eye hath not seen nor ear heard the things which God hath prepared for those that love him '(Corinthians 2:9). Both Tolstoy's dissertation and my own experience of meditation left me with a feeling that life offered no real hope of satisfying our deeply imbedded desire for survival, creating indeed a sense of hopeless futility. Indeed, it is possible to adopt the following cynical explanation of our strivings based solely on the traits of human nature —

(i)   Man, like the animals, is a product of the evolutionary struggle for survival and is engaged in a constant struggle to continue to survive.

(ii)   Systems of morality (such as, for example, the Ten Commandments) are created by Man as an aid to survival by promoting greater social harmony and a measure of justice.

(iii)   Having greater self-awareness than other animals and a related presentiment of the future Man is conscious of exercising a certain degree of control over his life and circumstances and instinctively wishes this state of affairs to continue. He therefore tends to invent belief in a supernatural Being to provide hope of an after-life and as something to " hang on to ", as it were, in the face of Life's vicissitudes. Such a belief also lends metaphysical support and vindication to his self-created systems of morality and law. It is also passed on from generation to generation by being inculcated in childhood, and the stronger this inculcation the stronger and more lasting its influence on a person's mind.

(iv)   In reality, however, in keeping with his evolutionary nature, Man is simply a part of a cellular continuum which is inevitably destined for dissolution and is therefore deluding himself as no future existence awaits him of the kind envisaged, the truth being contained, paradoxically, in a literal interpretation of Christ's claim that " God is the God of the living and not of the dead ." In the words of Omar Khayyam as translated by Edward Fitzgerald,

" One thing is certain, and the Rest is Lies ;

The Flower that once has blown for ever dies."

To state this thesis in concrete scientific terms, when one's heart stops beating, one's blood stops circulating with the result that one's brain stops functioning and cannot therefore be conscious of anything after this life.

Yet despite this counsel of despair we are still compelled to recognise one puzzling, unassailable fact — namely, the existence of the stellar conditions which made the evolution of life on our planet possible. I know of no-one, scientist or not, who can argue with the fact that there could have been no evolution without the existence of the Sun : stated in its simplest form — no Sun, no evolution ; and as we know that there are numerous Suns we may assert, I think, that our Sun did not *have* to exist. So why does it ? The scientific statement that it consists of ' nuclear reactions ' does not answer the question. Put another way, as it frequently has, why does anything exist ? Or as an 80-year old Servitor whom I can remember from my student days at Edinburgh University replied when asked if he believed in God " There had to be something before there could have been anything."

Students of philosophy will be familiar with how notoriously difficult it is to read and understand the writings of the German philosopher Hegel, particularly his major work *Phenomenology of Spirit*. I mention this because I have just been reading a guidebook to this work by Robert Stern and while doing so I have suddenly become aware, looking back on what I myself have written here, that I have to some extent been creating a succession of one-sided conceptual divisions or viewpoints of the sort which Hegel urges us to overcome by stepping back, as it were, and reflecting on the fact that some of the problems we pose have their source in a set of one-sided assumptions and are therefore pseudo-problems generated by our way of looking at the world rather than inherent in the world itself ; and according to Hegel, these can be resolved by a process of dialectical thinking which leads ordinary consciousness away from the oppositional thinking of the understanding and, by resolving certain dichotomies or ' blind spots ' in how we take the world to be, brings us back to our sense

that the world is a rational place in which our reason can feel truly
' at home '.

This outlook has served to heighten my consciousness of the fact
that I may have been guilty of adopting a one-sided epistemology
of what Stern conveniently describes as ' sense-certainty '. In fact,
at this stage of my *quaesitum* I had, in any case, wished to cast a
retrospective reflection on my strong argument in **2.** above (i.e. in
the section dealing with epistemology) that our knowledge of the
world was fundamentally based exclusively on sensory data . I am
aware in the first instance that I may have been wrong to contradict
Kant's notion of *a priori* intuition as a source of knowledge
independent of sense experience because I acknowledge the
possibility that after we have become aware of the existence of an
object *via* our senses we perhaps make a mental assumption as to
its causation that has not been prompted by our sensory recognition
of its existence. But the reader may recall that I attributed this
mental conception as having been subconsciously derived from the
sense experience encountered and absorbed during the process of
our evolution, and the reader can decide for himself whether this
resort to a scientific explanation is valid. But whatever the truth of
the position here I should like to stress that while I was previously
contending that our knowledge of the world was fundamentally
based on ' sense ' (i.e. on our sensory-data) I was not claiming
that it yielded us the other half of the coin, so to speak, namely,
' certainty ' as to the real underlying, or hidden, nature of the

' thing in itself ' even though my arguments may have seemed to be implying this.

By alluding to evolution in the above discussion it will be obvious that, rightly or wrongly, I am drawing on the evidence furnished by modern science into the controversy, and as Hegel clearly regarded his arguments as having the nature of ' Science ' and as promoting ' scientific insight ', it seems to me that I can do no better at this stage than turn to what purports to be the latest scientific understanding of our Universe as explained in a recent TV programme dealing with the intriguing issue of what modern scientists considered ' nothing ' to be. This began by relating the traditional view of ' nothing ' as expressed in Aristotle's well known assertion that " Nature abhors a vacuum ", implying that it was impossible to have a condition of nothingness. Then it pointed out that at a later stage in history it was found possible for Man to create a vacuum by filling a thin tube, or part of it, with mercury and then removing it from the tube. But scientists were still left wondering why light was able to pass through this vacuum if it was supposed to be truly ' nothingness '. Their answer at that stage took the form of an hypothesis that light was transmitted *via* a medium which filled the Universe outside our terrestrial sphere called the luminiferous *aether* or *ether* but the existence of the ether was later shown, courtesy of the Michelson-Morley experiment, to be inconsistent with Einstein's theory of special relativity involving the constancy of the velocity of light. Later still, in the 1920's, in trying to reconcile quantum mechanics with Einstein's special relativity theory, Paul Dirac, a Nobel Prize winning physicist, postulated the existence of anti-matter which has subsequently been confirmed. Each particle of matter has a corresponding particle of anti-matter with the same mass and spin but with an opposite electric charge and magnetic moment and which in collision will annihilate each other. The existence of our Universe was made possible by the fact that during the Big Bang more particles than anti-particles were produced, or at least persisted, the reason for this asymmetry being what scientists are currently striving to discover. In fact, in April this year, through the use of the Hadron Collider at CERN in Switzerland, scientists were able to trap anti-matter hydrogen particles for a longer period of time before extinction (about 17 minutes) than had hitherto been possible, opening up a prospect of being able to study them more closely in order to understand the rôle they played in the Big Bang.

Oddly enough, as it happens, I had no sooner decided to pursue these scientific revelations when I discovered that Hegel had cast doubt upon the ability of our consciousness to escape the puzzles that arise out of our ordinary conception of the world by moving to the ' scientific image ' of the world of physics which, in Hegel's time, was centred on the notion of force. According to Hegel, although the notion of force appears to surmount the aporia faced by the common-sense conception of things and properties, this

' scientific image ' of the world favoured by physics is also problematic because, by taking us too far away from the commonsense conception, it leads to a bifurcation in our world view concerning individuality and universality. As Stern's book explains, Hegel maintains in effect that once we go below the level of empirical phenomena it becomes harder to defend the claim that we have cognitive access to this underlying reality, or to know what we can say about it : and it thus becomes a ' super-sensible beyond ' outside the reach of our intellectual powers. Hegel claims that the scientific theorist cannot give us grounds for taking the world seriously from the ontological point of view unless he can give us grounds for taking this picture to be true ; but, he argues, how can such grounds be given, when we have gone beyond the direct evidence of the senses ? He thus distances himself from the then contemporary philosophical enthusiasm for the notion of force, trying to show that it is not possible to solve our philosophical difficulties simply by moving from the manifest to the scientific image.

It is difficult to avoid noticing how the above reference to a ' super-sensible beyond ' seems astonishingly close to the quantum world of modern physics in which sub-atomic particles behave in a seemingly random, non-rational manner. However, I would suggest that we are justified in claiming that Science has moved on somewhat since Hegel's day not only because it now supplies us with more verifiable evidence of its findings but also because, from the ontological point of view, it *does* furnish us with grounds for taking its picture to be true. In any case, it is the only avenue down which our insight into how our Universe came to be can advance, and I therefore propose to reflect on its implications. The conclusion drawn in the above-mentioned TV programme concerning how scientists regard the concept of ' nothing ' was that the initial vacuum or nothingness out of which our Universe emerged was " teeming with energy " and that this energy could be transformed into particles of matter provided the accompanying particles of anti-matter did not annihilate them. Since, for some reason, the latter became less numerous than the former the Universe had, according to the programme, apparently emerged out of nothing due to an inexplicably random undulation of energy, the energy explanation of its source being something which I had long since intuitively surmised. And when one can appreciate from Einstein's famous equation $E = mc^2$ that even a small amount of mass contains, potentially, an enormous quantity of energy we recognise that the entire Universe must therefore reflect a colossal amount of energy.

Let us suppose — as many of the modern scientists seem to imply — that the Big Bang which brought our Universe into being just happened by Chance. What is Chance ? A good definition that I recently came across *via* the internet reads as follows : ' the unknown and unpredictable element in happenings that seem to have no assignable cause. ', although it strikes me that some use of the word ' unintentional ' might have improved it. Viewed in these terms, inclusive of my addition, the Big Bang can probably be assumed to have had a cause but not a known or intended one. One thing about it, however, seems blatantly clear — namely, that if Space and Time did not exist prior to the event, then its occurrence would seem to have been a lot more unpredictable than would have been the case if they had. But if Science is really telling us that the original ' nothingness ' out of which the Universe sprang was " teeming with energy ", then, contrary to its own current teaching, it seems highly probable that Space and Time did in fact exist *before* the Big Bang, making it seem slightly less likely that that the latter could have occurred by ' accident ' simply because it would have had to have happened at a particular, and therefore, a possibly designated, point in time.

At this point I am reminded of a question my mother used to pose in a rhetorical vein — namely, where did the sea come from ? It's a very good question, but wherever it came from, anyone with a sailor's experience of the sea will be aware of the mighty energy contained in it, and this represents only a miniscule fraction of the energy inherent in the mass of the entire Universe. For me, this energy is the creative Spirit or ' God ' we all seem to be pondering about, although, unlike Richard Dawkins and David Attenborough apparently, I have philosophical problems with the notion that its transformation into the visible substance of our Universe simply " happened " without the deliberate action of an invisible, indetectible will. Indeed, it seems to me that we have come full circle, as it were, and that there is still a strong probability that we are back with the Christian notion that the Almighty created the Universe out of nothing in a rather similar sense to that conveyed by the Biblical sentence " Let there be light, and there was light." At the very least, scientists such as Richard Dawkins have not yet proved otherwise.

In fact, the entire search in which we have been engaged seems to leave us in a somewhat similar position to that expressed below in Quatrain 27 of Edward Fitzgerald's first translation of the Rubaiyat of Omar Khayyám —

" Myself when young did eagerly frequent
  Doctor and Saint, and heard great Argument
  About it and about ; but evermore
  Came out by the same Door as in I went. "

Indeed, I venture to suggest that not even the possible discovery of the Higgs particle, which is the one described as the ' God particle ' because it is thought to have been the original source of the mass of all the other detectible particles, will alter the fact that we are here confronted with a mystery which our finite minds are still unable to comprehend and may never be able to. Neither my philosophical ponderings nor the latest scientific findings have so far given me convincing cause to contradict the concept dogmatically expressed in the Westminster Shorter Catechism adopted by the Church of Scotland in the words " God is a Spirit, infinite, eternal, and unchangeable " or the transcendental, devotional aspect of the following words from the Liturgy of the Scottish Episcopal Church : " The Lord is a great God, and a great King above all Gods ; in His hand are the four corners of the Earth ; and the strength of the hills is His also. "

Index

Aether, ether, the luminiferous 48

Allen, Dave 1

' Anthropic principle ', the 34-36

Anti-matter particles 49

Aristotle 48

Arnold, Matthew , quote from, 26

Attenborough, David 52

Babylonians 2

Beethhoven 40-41

Berkeley, Bishop 23

Bible, the 1, 2, 3

Big Bang, the 4, 19, 28-29, 39, 49, 51-52

Black Holes 20

Cartesian dualism 12

CERN 20, 49

Chance 51

Christ, Jesus 42, 45

Christianity 21,

Churchill, Winston 21

Church of Scotland, the 53

Dark Matter and Energy 29

Darwinism 36

Dawkins, Richard 4, 27-28, *The God Delusion,*
     29, 32, 34-36, 38-41, 52-53

Dialectical thinking 46

Dirac, Paul 49

Einstein 23, 48, 51 ($E = mc^2$)

Epistemology 6

Euclid 34

Evolution/evolutionary 4, 11,
     14, 35-36, 44, 45, 47, 48

Findlay, J. N. 33

Fitzgerald, Edward 45, 53

Frege, Gottlob 8-9, 23

Genesis 2, 4

Gideon, Bible the 1

' Goldilocks zone ', the 35

Hadron, Collider, the 20, 49

Hawkings, Stephen 29

Hegel, G.W.F. 33, 46,
     Phenomenology of Spirit ,
     48-50

Higgs boson particle, the 19, 53

Hitler, Adolph 21

Hobbs, Thomas 26

Hume, David i, 6-7

Kant, Emmanuel 10, *Critique
     of Pure Reason*, 11, 14,
     Forms of Intuition, 47

Khayyam, Omar 45, 53,

Index (cont'd)

Logical Atomism 16-17

Logical Positivism/Positivists 17, 20
   24

'Maranatha ' 43

Marlowe, Christopher 41

Michelson-Morley experiment, the 48

Mill, John Stuart 6

Moses 3

Newman, John Henry 6

Ontology 18

Plato 37 (see *footnote*)

' Principle of sufficient reason ', the 38

Russell, Bertrand 16-18, *Principia Mathematica,* 21-22

Sartre, Jean-Paul 15, 21

Schopenhauer, Alfred 14, 36-38, *The World as Will and Representation*

Science, scientific 3, 4, 7, 10, 11, 17, 19, 23-25, 30, 32-33, 37-39, 45-50, 52-53

(pages on which either or

   both words appear)

Shakespeare 40-41

Spinoza 27, 34, 42

Stern, Robert 46, 47, 50

St.Paul 21

String Theory 32

Sub-atomic particles, 23, 30, 50

Ten Commandments, the 3, 44

Theology, Professor of 41

Tolstoy, Leo 42, *The Gospel in Brief,* 44

Universe, the 3, 7, 19, 24-27, 32, 34-36, 38-42, 48, 49, 51-53

    (pages on which references to
    the word appear)

Verifiability Criterion of Meaning, the 24

Vienna Circle 17, 19, 20

Westminster Shorter Catechism, the 39, 53

Wittgenstein 10, 13, 24 *Tractatus — Logico Philosophicus,* 17, his Picture Theory, 22

THE END

www.ingramcontent.com/pod-product-compliance
Lightning Source LLC
Chambersburg PA
CBHW021223020426
42331CB00003B/443